Bunny Yeager's
Flirts of the

Schiffer Publishing Ltd

4880 LOWER VALLEY ROAD ATGLEN, PENNSYLVANIA 19310

Other books by Bunny Yeager

Photographing Girls in Jamaica
Bunny's Bikini Beauties
Bunny's Honeys
Bettie Page Confidential
How I Photograph Nudes
How I Photograph Myself
100 Girls
Camera in the Caribbean
Camera in Mexico
Camera in Jamaica
Bunny Yeager's New Photo Discoveries
Bunny Yeager's Famous Models
Fifty New Models
How to Take Figure Photos
Bunny Yeager's Photo Studies

How to Photograph the Figure
ABC's of Figure Photography
The Art of Glamour Photography
Photographing the Female Figure
Drawing the Human Figure Using Photographs
Bunny Yeager's Postcard Book
Bunny Yeager's Bikini Girls of the 1950s
Bikini Girls of the 1960s
Bunny Yeager's Pin-Up Girls of the 1950s
Bunny Yeager's Pin-Up Girls of the 1960s

For information about ordering photographs by Bunny Yeager, write to her at 9301 NE 6 Avenue, Suite B201, Miami, FL 33138 or at bunnyyeager@aol.com. Her telephone number is 305-757-8978. Visit her website at bunnyyeager.com.

Cover photo:
Cover girl is Maria Stinger, known as Miami's Marilyn Monroe. When the movie Seven Year Itch was released, the theater promoted it by having a "look-alike" beauty contest. Maria won it.

Title page photo:
Bunny Yeager applies make-up to Carolyn Kelly before shooting on location. See Carolyn in action on page 89.

Designed by John P. Cheek
Cover design by Bruce Waters
Type set in Korinna BT

ISBN: 978-0-7643-2637-0
Printed in China

Published by Schiffer Publishing Ltd.
4880 Lower Valley Road
Atglen, PA 19310
Phone: (610) 593-1777; Fax: (610) 593-2002
E-mail: Info@schifferbooks.com

For the largest selection of fine reference books on this and related subjects, please visit our web site at
www.schifferbooks.com
We are always looking for people to write books on new and related subjects. If you have an idea for a book please contact us at the above address.

This book may be purchased from the publisher.
Include $3.95 for shipping.
Please try your bookstore first.
You may write for a free catalog.

In Europe, Schiffer books are distributed by
Bushwood Books
6 Marksbury Ave.
Kew Gardens
Surrey TW9 4JF England
Phone: 44 (0) 20 8392-8585;
Fax: 44 (0) 20 8392-9876
E-mail: info@bushwoodbooks.co.uk
Website: www.bushwoodbooks.co.uk
Free postage in the U.K., Europe; air mail at cost.

Bunny Yeager,
Photographer and Model

It may look like flirting when Bunny sets up her camera on a tripod with a mirror beside it
while she goes into various posing positions to take her own photo but she is not. She has
careully selected a location where there is no one around. (Unless it is a "peeping Tom"!)

Contents

Introduction
Tina Skinner

Bunny Yeager's name is synonymous with the glamorous, playful pin-up girls of the 1950s. She worked both ends of the camera, launching her career as a beauty queen and model, and then taking control of the shutter to become one of America's best-known photographers.

As a beauty contestant, her achievements included the crown of Miami Sports Queen in 1949, with a trophy presented by baseball star Joe DiMaggio. She went on to become one of the most popular Florida pin-up models of the 1950s, and appeared in Playboy. It wasn't long, however, before she started creating her own celebrities. Her subjects included Bettie Page, and Yeager's work was greatly responsible for that that pop icon's success.

Yeager was proclaimed "The World's Prettiest Photographer" in 1953 by U.S. Camera magazine, and in

Bunny working with Mary Poole on beach

1959 she was chosen as Photographer of the Year. She has published numerous books of her photographs.

Recently, Yeager was featured in a CNN story about the 60th anniversary of the bikini. Her many talents include sewing, and she often created the bikinis her subjects modeled for photographs.

Yeager was at her best photographing full-figured women cavorting in the Florida sun. Her dramatic settings often involve the surf and sand of her hometown, Miami. And her early work is evocative of an era of flirtatious innocence. This book explores the themes of "flirty" and "fifties" as they came to symbolize femininity in the midst of the 20th century.

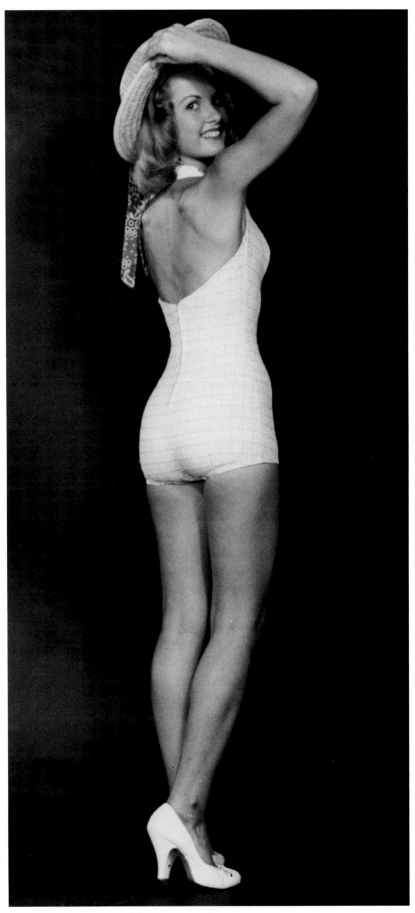

Alice Lightbourne

Maria Stinger

Lana Bashama

Dolly Doyle

Nadine Ducas

Una Diehl

Bettie Page

Linda Vargas

Lisa Winters

Allison Hayes

Jenny Lee

Joyce Nizzari

Claudia Randall

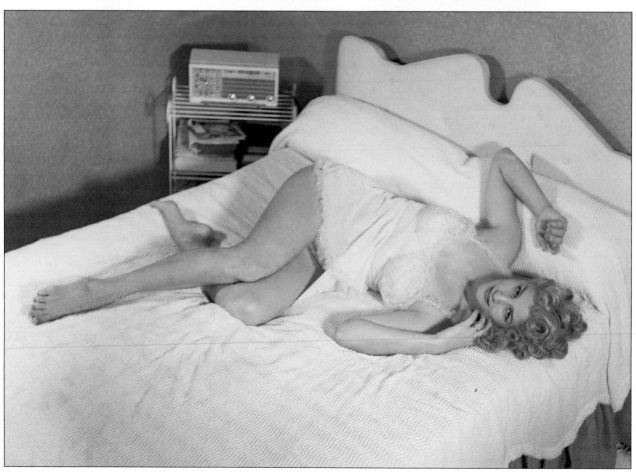

Kathleen Stanley

Evelyn West

Lynn Lyckles

Cindy Fuller

Tammy Edwards

Myrna Weber

Elaine Beatty

Lynn Brooks

Denise Lamont

Candy Tint

La Raine Meeres

Louise Rogers

Carol Blake

Nanci De Celle

Dolores Carlos

Virginia Booker

Susan Scott

Diane Webber

Joyce Russell

Chris Darling

Pat Stanford

Carol Jean Lauritzen

Carrie Price

Nina Coral

Ruth Shepard

44

Yvonne Fredricks

Mary Flynn

Jeanne Gallagher

Bibi Grante

Sheryl Parks

Chris Mara

Scodie Hull

Marlayna Scott

Terry Shaw

Phyllis Ursin

Pat Gardner

Pat Cooper

Janet Johnson

Jayne Hartwell

Jackie Walker

Nikki Wyatt

Dodie Mitchell

Florence Harrell

Ginger Martin

Rochelle Gallucci

Peggy Jackson

Val Ritchie

Alta Whipple

Inez Pinchot

Sara Brockett

Sally Larimer

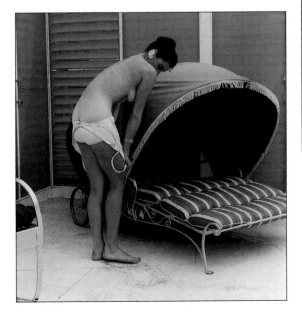

Rita Ramsey

Linda Laine

Anita Mc Crea

Diane Wagner

Mara Lindsey

Pat Simmons

Sharon Lee

Lori Shea

Dolores Hodges

Sue James

Mary Ann Harrison

Sharon Knight

Teri Hope

Marcella Patrick

Jane Millar

Barbara Karwath

Jackie Miller

Virginia Remo

Carolyn Kelly

Patti Simmons

Marcella Hansen

Melody West

Lacey Kelly

Carol Paullus

Joan Sherwood

Dolly Murcia

Helene Aimee

Mary Tilghman

Charlene Mathies

Yvonne Menard

Maritza Antoinette

Micki Marlo

Eleanor Lucky

Sandy Fulton

Nanci White

Patti Patelle

Kevin Cornell

Mary Mills

Lillian Balikian

Julia Saxon

Paula Casey

Ann Brockway

Marge Hershey

107

Gigi Reynolds

Louise Whitney

Tina Tiffany

Jet Hamrin

Cindy Lee

Rebel Rawlings

Billie Sue Hunzicker

Julie Padilla

Joyce George

Gloria Sheridan

Olga Chaviano

Dixie Evans

Marcia Valibus

Joan Rawlings

Carolyn Lee

Joan Lamb

Natalie Tokare

Della Vaughn

Audi Ragona

Joyce Miles

Joy Murphy

Dottie Sykes

Kelly Evans

Lynn Tracy

Suzi Marshall

Betty Johnson

Joan Chewning

Dominique Chappelle

Camille Stewart

San San

Dondi Penn

Carol Britt

Lillian Bell

Ann Cummings

Irene Twinam

Bunny Yeager,
Photographer and Model

Bunny Yeager

Bunny Yeager

Alphabetical Index